Cognitive Behavioral Therapy

For All Mood Disorders and Addictions

Jim Berry

Table of Contents

1: What is Cognitive Behavioral Therapy?

2: When Cognitive Behavioral Therapy is used

3: Cognitive Behavioral Therapy Sessions

4: How to Apply CBT in Your Life

5: How to Change Your Thoughts

6: How to Change Your Behavior

7: Overcoming Mood Disorders and Addictions

8: Changing Your Perspective

9: Adopting Lifestyle Changes to prevent a Relapse

Conclusion

Introduction

If you have mood disorders and addictions, this book will help you to overcome them and live a meaningful life. This is a practical cognitive behavioral therapy CBT self-help book which will help you to understand yourself and gain knowledge of how to overcome your problems.

After reading and applying the recommendations in this book, you will begin to change your thoughts and behaviors to make yourself feel better. Cognitive behavioral therapy is one of the most effective therapies that have been developed to treat mental illnesses and substance addictions. The principles in this book can be practiced on a daily basis and will live on with the patient, even after the treatment is completed.

This is a valuable book which will help you to overcome anxiety, depression, phobias, panic attacks, obsessive compulsive behavior, drug and alcohol addictions, and all other mood disorders and addictions. CBT is a talking therapy that will help you manage your problems by changing the way you think and behave. Unlike other talking treatments, CBT deals with your current problems rather than focusing on issues from your past. It looks for practical ways to improve your state of mind on a daily basis.

This is a book that explores what CBT is and when it is used, what to expect from therapy sessions, how to apply CBT in your life and how to change your thoughts and behaviors to be able to overcome mood disorders and addictions. The skills and procedures you'll learn will help you prevent a relapse that will stay with you for the rest of your life.

1: What is Cognitive Behavioral Therapy?

Cognitive behavioral therapy (CBT) is a type of psychotherapy or talking treatment which is used to treat mood disorders and addictions. This therapy was originally developed for treating anxiety and depression, but today it is used to treat a wide-range of mental illnesses and physical health problems.

CBT is based on the concept that, your thoughts, feelings (emotions and physical sensations) and actions are interconnected and they affect each other. Negative thoughts and feelings lead to negative behavior forming patterns which can trap you in a vicious cycle. CBT aims to help you crack this vicious cycle by breaking down overwhelming problems into smaller parts and showing you how to change the negative patterns to improve the way you feel.

There are links between what you feel and think and what you do. The way you think about yourself, other people, situations and the world has a lot to do with your actions.

- *Cognitive means the way we feel and think*
- *Behavior means the way we act or behave*

Cognitive behavioral therapy is a talking therapy used by trained therapists to help patients manage their difficulties. This is done by changing the way they feel and think (Cognitive) and the way they behave (behavior).

How does CBT help?

CBT is most commonly used to treat anxiety and depression, but it is useful in the treatment of all mood disorders and addictions. CBT will help you deal with your problems in a more positive way so you can overcome them completely. Take for example, anxiety. This is a natural emotion you feel time and again.

The therapists conducting cognitive behavioral therapy will focus on examining the relationship between their patients' thoughts, feelings and behaviors. They explore the patterns of thinking that lead the patient to self-destructive feelings and behaviors. They know that, thoughts and feelings are the main contributory factors to actions.

Therapists will try to find out about the patients' belief systems because this is very powerful in directing thoughts, either positively or negatively. If patients with mental problems are helped to modify their patterns of thinking, it improves their coping mechanisms, whether they are faced with anxiety, phobia, addictions or other problems.

Difference between CBT and traditional psychotherapy

CBT is different from traditional psychotherapy. The therapist and the patient actively work together on one-on-one sessions or with family or groups, to help the patient to recover. However, for CBT to be effective and have long-lasting effects, the patient is actively involved.

There is no way that it can work without the patient playing his or her role. It is therefore very interactive and the patient involved will be given activities that are analyzed before new activities are developed.

This therapy is based on the concept that patient's thoughts, feelings and actions are all interconnected in a way. Negative thoughts and feelings trap patients into a vicious cycle that is hard to break out. The therapist aim is to help patients break out of this cycle and become free from controlled mood swings and addictions.

If you are suffering from any mood disorder or addictions, the therapist will help you break down the problem into smaller parts which then can be dealt with when you are able to change the negative patterns to improve your feelings.

CBT deals with current problems

CBT is different from other talking treatments because it addresses your current problems. Many therapies focus on past issues to find the root cause of the problem, but CBT is used to solve current problems. It helps to change your current thinking and behavior in positive ways. There is nothing wrong in talking about the past and how it has affected your life, but CBT focuses on the present moment. It focuses on improving your current mental well-being and not what you have gone through in the past. You can practice what has been recommended in this book to break away from your unhelpful habits, or you can work with your therapist to find practical ways to improve your thinking and feelings, ultimately leading to positive behavior or actions. CBT is effective when done on a daily basis.

When Cognitive behavioral therapy can be used

Scientific studies conducted have demonstrated that CBT has been successful in the treatment of a wide range of mental and physical problems which include:

- mood disorders
- anxiety disorders
- eating disorders
- sleep disorders
- personality disorders
- substance abuse disorders
- psychotic disorders and many other health problems

The research studies have shown that cognitive behavioral therapy changes the brain activity in patients with mood disorders and addictions who have received this treatment. It shows that brain functions better after the therapy and the patient feels a lot better, eventually breaking free from all addictions.

Benefits of Cognitive Behavioral Therapy CBT

1. Cognitive behavioral therapy is highly structured. It is available in many forms such as one-on-one sessions, family and group therapy, computerized behavioral therapy, and even self-help books.

2. Cognitive behavioral therapy can be more effective than medication when it is used to treat mood disorders and addictions like anxiety, depression and phobias. However, patients must be committed to the process.

3. CBT may be helpful where medications have failed to work on their own. It can be used alone or combined with medications depending on the severity of the problem.

4. CBT deals with current problems and therefore become effective within a relatively short period of time compared to other talking therapies.

5. The recommendations in this book concerning CBT are helpful, practical and effective. You should practice them regularly to prevent lapses and relapses.

2: When Cognitive Behavioral Therapy is used

CBT can be used in any type of mood disorder, relationship problems, physical problems, drug and alcohol addictions and mental illnesses.

However, there are some severe conditions which require medications. In some cases, you need you to consult specialists.

Types of CBT

CBT can be carried out in different forms which include:

- *Individual therapy* – involves one-on-one sessions with a trained therapist.
- *Family therapy* – involves you and members of your family.
- *Group therapy* – is provided with other people who have similar problems.
- *Computer-based programs* – is known as computerized cognitive behavioral therapy (CCBT).

You may choose one of these forms or combine several of them altogether. You can also start with one type and proceed with the other one as you prefer.

Conditions treated with CBT

CBT is used to treat various conditions. These include:

- anxiety disorders
- depression
- post-traumatic stress disorder (PTSD)
- panic disorders
- phobias
- obsessive compulsive disorder (OCD)
- insomnia and other sleeping disorders
- anorexia and bulimia among other eating disorders
- problems related to drug and alcohol misuse
- relationship problems

CBT can help you deal with these conditions until you are able to overcome them permanently.

In adults, CBT has been used to treat many conditions such as anxiety disorders, depression, sleeping disorders, eating disorders, phobia, obsessive compulsive disorders, post-traumatic stress disorders and substance-use disorders with great success. It also plays a role in the treatment of low back pain, personality disorders, schizophrenia and psychosis. CBT is also used to overcome spinal cord injuries, fibromyalgia and other health conditions. It is effectively used to treat insomnia instead of sleeping pills.

In children and adolescents, CBT is used as an effective treatment of anxiety, depression, suicidal tendencies, eating disorders and obesity, post-traumatic stress disorder, obsessive compulsive disorder and many repetitive disorders. Suicidal prevention CBT-SP has been developed to treat the adolescents with severe depression who may have attempted suicide. It is known to be effective and acceptable.

In addition to these programs, there are CBT video games which are used to help young people resolve their own problems without getting overwhelmed by them. These methods are found to be quite effective, especially when they are applied by children and teenagers.

How cognitive behavioral therapy works:

Whether you are working on addictions, moods or other problems, the therapist breaks down cognitive behavioral therapy into five main areas.

1. Situations
2. Thoughts
3. Physical feelings
4. Emotions
5. Actions or behavior

Cognitive behavioral therapy is based on these 5 main areas. These five factors of CBT are interconnected. A situation may arise in which you interpret or attach meaning to a certain incident. The thoughts you have about this situation usually affect your physical feelings and emotions which leads to your actions. If your thoughts about yourself, others and situations are negative then your feelings and actions will be affected negatively. Do you see the pattern?

How to stop the negative cycle

We all respond to situations in ways that are either helpful or unhelpful. The way people interpret a situation or the meaning they give to it, is what causes feelings and emotions. If something bad happens to you at a given time, you may feel angry, sad, lonely, hopeless, guilty or depressed.

The way you respond to certain situations depends on whether you have positive or negative thoughts about those situations. If these negative feelings and emotions are not dealt with in a positive way, they may be followed by negative actions like withdrawal from people, violence, self-hate, addictions and other problems.

When you are trapped in such negative thoughts, your actions make you feel even worse and this makes the situation worse, and the whole scenario repeats itself. But should you allow this to go on and on? No. If we allow this to go on, we allow things to go out of control as we go on a downward spiral. Even when you don't believe it, just know that you have power over it. You can stop the downward spiral and turn it around to your benefit.

Most of what we go through in life is not about what happens to us but how we react to the situation. There are many things that are beyond our control such as earthquakes, weather conditions, accidents, fire, and diseases. Even situations that are within our control don't always go smoothly. We are left feeling guilty, scared, anxious, depressed, tired, and frustrated.

At times people take drugs and alcohol to escape from reality and before they know it they have become addicts. Some puff a cigarette and before they know it, they are hooked. Think of situations you have experienced that have made you to feel the way you do and write them down.

How CBT helps you
In any situation, CBT helps you to be in control by changing what you think, which changes what you do, which changes how you feel. It can change negative thoughts to positive thoughts which lead to positive actions helping you feel better.

CBT aims to break down those things that make you acquire negative thoughts and emotions so you can stop feeling the way you do. It helps your problems more manageable.

3: Cognitive Behavioral Therapy Sessions

Cognitive behavioral therapy can be provided by a trained therapist in one-on-one sessions between the patient and the therapist. Family members like your mother, father, sibling or spouse can accompany you so they can help you to manage the problem.

Furthermore, problems affect the whole family so it is important to get help as a family. It makes you accountable for your actions. You will stay focused on your goals to improve your mood swings and additions.

The therapist will give you sessions which last 30-60 minutes depending on the severity of the problem although group sessions can take 2 ½ hours or longer. Exposure therapy sessions usually take much longer to ensure that your anxiety has significantly reduced during each session.

Therapy can take place in the therapist's clinic, your home, if you have obsessive compulsive disorder or agoraphobia of specific things at home such as the stairs, pets or the darkness, or you can have it outside if you have phobias or fears of things that are outside, like swimming pools, spiders and animals. Your therapist can be a healthcare professional who has been specifically trained in CBT such as a psychologist, a psychiatrist or a General Physician, or it can be a psychiatric nurse.

The first CBT session

Therapy starts with initial assessment of your condition. During the first few sessions, the CBT therapist will ask you or your family member questions to determine whether CBT is the right therapy for you at that moment. This also helps him or her to know that you will be comfortable with this process.

The therapist will ask you questions about:

- your life and your background
- your belief systems such as childhood upbringing, family values, past experiences
- whether you are anxious or depressed
- your phobias, addictions, insomnia, OCD
- whether your condition interferes with your family, work, and your social life
- events and situations that may be related to your condition
- treatments you may have had and their effectiveness
- what you intend to achieve with CBT therapy

If CBT seems to be the appropriate treatment for you, the therapist will explain what to expect from this treatment and will make arrangements for a face-to-face therapy sessions. You will have one session each week or each night up to 5-20 sessions depending on your condition. Some therapists recommend 5-20 sessions while others recommend 6-18 sessions, but you can always have a booster when you need further therapy. Each session will last for about 30-60 minutes and you will have "breaks" of 1-3 weeks between sessions when you can do your "homework" assignments.

The assignment may be a simple one like facing your fears for someone with phobia or attending a social event for someone who is depressed or anxious.

Completing the assignment shows how dedicated you are to the treatment. If you have the desire to change then you will achieve the goals you have set. After completion your assignment and evaluating how successful you were, the therapist will plan the next session. During "breaks" it may help to have real time counseling with your therapist through computer links or over the phone.

If this type of therapy is not appropriate for you or you don't feel comfortable receiving it, the therapist may recommend alternative therapies and treatments.

Follow-up sessions

Immediately after the assessment sessions, your therapist will start working with you as an individual or as a group to break down your problems into situations, thoughts, emotions, physical feelings and actions as we have seen earlier. You may be asked to write down on a diary about your thoughts and behaviors to see the patterns they form.

You and your therapist will work together to analyze your thoughts, feelings and behaviors (actions) to see if they are unrealistic, irrational or unhelpful thoughts. Together, you will check and see how your thoughts, feelings and behaviors are interconnected and how they affect each other, how they affect you and others around you, such as family and colleagues. Your therapist will help you to change your unhelpful thoughts and behaviors and replace them with alternative thoughts which are helpful.

What to expect during CBT sessions

Effective cognitive behavioral therapy depends on how successful the healthcare provider and the patient interact. CBT is unlike other forms of psychotherapy because the patient is very involved. The homework assignment should start with simple things before moving to more difficult assignments. You should work at easier assignment first so you can feel comfortable with the process.

The changes you have made will be measured to know the effectiveness of the therapy. After making changes to your thoughts and behavior, your therapist will ask you to practice using them in your daily life.

After few sessions, you should challenge upsetting thoughts and replace them with alternative thoughts which are helpful. Keep practicing until you recognize you are about to do something that is irrational, which will ultimately make you feel bad. Correct this potential behavior by doing something that is helpful, and this will make you feel better. This will motivate you even more to change your thoughts and actions and you will feel better and better.

You will do more "homework" assignments between CBT sessions moving to more and more difficult scenarios. During each session, you will need to discuss with your therapist about the changes you have made and how it felt. Your therapist will make suggestions to help you with the process.

Exposure therapy can be difficult at first when you start confronting your fears and anxieties. If you fear spiders, you can start by looking at their pictures. Later, you can watch them in enclosed places if you are able to cope with it. Your therapist will not in any way ask you to do things that you don't want to do.

You will work at the pace that you are comfortable with. During the CBT sessions, whether you are working as an individual or as a group, your therapist will encourage and reassure you until you are quite comfortable with the treatment progress.

One of the benefits of CBT is that, after you have completed your course, you will be able to continue to apply the skills and the principles that you have learned in your daily life. When you do this regularly, you will prevent a relapse and ensure that the symptoms do not return. This should help you to manage your mood disorders and addictions and stop them from controlling your life and having a negative impact on you and others.

Computerized Cognitive Behavioral Therapy (CCBT)

Advancement of technology and the internet have ensured that there are a number of interactive software programs that are available today that you can use without the help of a therapist. The computer packages have been effective in the treatment of mild to moderate mood disorders and addictions, although the programs work better when they are taken with support. Supporters make you feel accountable to them than having to do the therapy all by yourself.

Sometimes computerized cognitive behavioral therapy is preferred instead of face-to-face sessions because it is a private therapy and it is cost-effective. This is also known as internet-delivered cognitive behavioral therapy (ICBT).

Computerized cognitive behavioral therapy improves your access to evidence-based CBT therapies and overcomes the prohibitive costs of face-to-face therapy and lack of availability of affordable professional therapists.

4: How to Apply CBT in Your Life

Cognitive behavioral therapy (CBT) is referred to as a self-help guide for mild to moderate mental and physical disorders. In self-help therapy, you need to recognize what the problem is and have the desire to overcome it.

In addition to cognitive behavioral therapy, many people with mental and health problems benefit from making lifestyle changes such as exercising regularly, avoiding or minimizing alcohol intake and avoiding smoking.

You can apply CBT in your life in four steps:

1. Identify thoughts, feelings and behaviors
2. Understand the links between thoughts, feelings and behaviors
3. Challenge your thoughts
4. Make changes to your thoughts and behaviors

Step 1: Identify thoughts, feelings and behaviors

To overcome mood disorders and addictions, you need to identify your thoughts, feelings (both emotions and physical sensations) and behaviors. This is due to the fact that, thoughts lead to feelings which lead to behaviors. These behaviors lead to thoughts which again lead to feelings and the whole pattern is repeated over and over again. This becomes a vicious cycle as explained earlier in

Chapter 1. Thoughts, feelings and behaviors are linked or interconnected to each other and each one of them has a way of affecting the others.

Anxiety

Anxiety is a normal emotion which we feel from time to time. We feel anxious when we have to sit for an exam, attend an interview and when we have a sick child. This is normal and we don't have to worry about it. However, persistent anxiety causes overwhelming fear or worry which can range from mild to severe. CBT is successful in treating persistent anxiety. This is not a one and done emotional therapy expecting it will go away on its own. There are people who experience constant fear and worry about various events and situations, which may lead to general anxiety disorder (GAD).

General anxiety disorder can cause mental and physical ailment which may interfere with your life making it hard for you to relax. Other people suffer from phobias, panic attacks, post-traumatic stress disorder (PTSD), obsessive compulsive behavior and social anxiety disorder, all of which have anxiety as one of the symptoms. All these conditions can affect your daily life in one way or another and cause distress. This is why it needs to be treated as early as possible.

If you are suffering from anxiety, identify the thoughts, feelings and behavior.

Identify thoughts:

- I am in danger
- things will go wrong
- I will not be able to cope with what happens
- what shall I do

There could be real danger or imagined danger. Both can make you anxious. For real danger you need to make wise decisions while for imagined danger you need to replace your thoughts with helpful ones.

Identify feelings:

- Heart races: the adrenaline rush makes your heart race faster. The blood flows into the arms ready to fight, into the legs ready to flight and into the lungs to help you breathe, as you fight-or-flight.

- Breathe faster: the breathing helps to transport the blood to where it is needed most; arms, legs and lungs.

- Sweating: you start to sweat as the body releases fluids to help it cool down.

- Muscles tense up: ready to fight or flight. You may have chest pains, dizziness and fatigue.

Identify behavior:

You may fight, flight or freeze. You could use your thoughts to overestimate (exaggerate) the danger and underestimate your coping ability.

You can apply this method to any type of problem.

Depression

Depression is constant sadness, hopelessness and loss of interest in things you used to enjoy. Fortunately, if you have depression and you receive the right treatment, you can go all the way to full recovery. CBT is an effective way of treating depression with or without a therapist. CBT can be combined with medications in treating severe cases of depression.
You may think:

- "I am hopeless"
- "People hate me"
- "I am good for nothing" and other unhelpful thoughts.

You may feel:

- Hopeless
- Sad

- Worthless
- Suicidal

You may behave:

- fail to go to work
- Sleep all day

Step 2: Understand the links between thoughts, feelings and behaviors

Anxiety

When you sense you are in danger, you feel anxious. In such situations you get a fight-or-flight response when your adrenaline rises. This is a life-saving response whether the danger you face is real or imagined. It is okay when the danger is real because you either fight it or run to safety. But when the danger is imagery in your head, it can cause extreme In fact, you look around for any signals that indicate you might be in danger.

Step 3 Make changes to your thoughts and behavior

CBT is a short-term psychotherapy treatment method which is goal-oriented. It aims at changing patterns of thinking and/or behavior to make people feel better. It helps you tackle the difficulties you are encountering. You can apply this treatment by focusing on changing your attitudes, beliefs and image of yourself. It can solve your emotional problems, relationship problems, and drug and alcohol addictions.

CBT is based on the model, "it is not the events and situations you go through that upsets you, but the meanings you give them." If your thoughts are negative, they block your mind from seeing things the way they are. You need to change your thoughts and behaviors as we shall see in Chapters 5 and 6.

Step 4 Challenge your thoughts

Therapist will help you to dispel these distorted thoughts and ask you to challenge these beliefs either in real life or as a hypothesis. You are encouraged to write down automatic thoughts which pop up in your mind. You will be monitored so they do not lead to negative feelings and self-destructive behaviors. You may not be aware of these automatic thoughts but once you start writing them down in your diary, it becomes easier for you to identify and report them. This is a key factor in overcoming your difficulties.

Therapists will also help you to develop realistic meanings or interpretations of events and situations. You are encouraged to depend on facts that have some kind of evidence instead of opinions that may have been overlooked as evidence.

CBT is a combination of both psychotherapy and behavioral therapy. Psychotherapy places great emphasis on the importance of personal meanings we attach to certain things. Behavioral therapy looks at the relationship between the problems you have, your behavior and your thoughts. CBT has gained popularity among therapists and patients because of its ability to treat mental illness. It is therefore practiced by GPs, psychologists, psychiatrists, social workers and nurses who have trained in CBT.

5: How to Change Your Thoughts

Cognitive therapy is based on the concept that, what we feel is mainly determined by our thinking. Many disorders are believed to be formed by faulty thoughts and beliefs. However, this can be corrected to improve moods and emotions. For example, research studies have shown that depressed people often have inaccurate and incorrect beliefs about themselves, their situations and the world at large. Common cognitive errors include:

- **Personalization** - becoming too personal by relating negative events and situations to you without any basis for this

- **Selective abstraction** - focusing your attention only on negative aspects instead of looking at the "big picture"

- **Dichotomous thinking** - viewing things in one way only, without looking at other perspectives

- **Magnification and minimization** – exaggerating the problem and minimizing your belief in your ability to cope with the situation, instead of being realistic or rational

Cognitive therapists will work with you to challenge your thinking. The therapist points out other alternative ways of viewing the same situation, giving you a wider view of yourself and life in general, which ultimately improves your moods.

Thoughts

Feelings are made up of both physical sensations and emotions. When your heart races and you breathe faster due to fight-or-flight response, your muscles tighten up and you get palpitations, chest pains, muscle aches and pains, these are known as physical sensations.

Behaviors

Most of our feelings are reflex actions. This means that our reactions happen automatically. Many times we do not consider our actions or the consequences when we react. We just do what comes naturally and it may not be the right thing if your thoughts are distorted. This is why you should think before you leap. You can only control the way you feel if you change your thoughts, behaviors, or actions. We have a choice.

If you feel like screaming you don't have to scream. If you feel like fighting you don't have to. You don't have to smoke or drink alcohol because you can control your thoughts and your actions in positive ways.

CBT helps you to consider your thoughts and actions and the effect they have on your feelings.

Many times we assume we cannot control our thoughts because they come automatically. To some extent that is true. But, we can control how we react to those thoughts.

How to change thoughts

It is true that you cannot stop your thoughts from coming but you have choices about how you react to them. CBT will help you to act differently to thoughts, making you react in helpful ways and ultimately lead to helpful thoughts.

Thoughts come naturally and when they upset you, you can respond by reacting to them. This makes you feel worse and worse. You can choose not to react to them out of your own free will. Dismiss negative thoughts. If you do, they will have no power over you.

Learn how to challenge your thoughts instead of believing them and doing what they want. You can focus your attention on positive things instead of reacting to unhelpful thoughts. CBT helps you to break unhelpful thinking habits. Write those unhelpful thinking habits down and choose how you will think differently. As you practice, you will find it easier to act rationally and feel better which affects your thoughts. That is how you change your thoughts.

How to change anger thoughts

You can change your anger thoughts. It is like when someone speaks to you rudely. Take for example something like "You are ugly" You have many choices.

Choice 1:

You can react by becoming angry and feeling humiliated. You may choose to hit back the same way, by being rude also to that person. This makes the other person hit back again even with more nasty things which makes you feel even worse. The attacker uses your emotions as a way of entertainment. But wait a minute; do you believe you are what he said….ugly? If you do, you will react with more anger and this will make you feel worse. These thoughts will make you act in unhelpful ways which lead to more negative thoughts even as the bully keeps targeting you. Does it help you? No.

Choice 2:

You can say something that will keep off the bully like how you topped him in class in the last exam.

Use a fact that he knows too well. He will shy away and stop his bullying. If he tries other methods use more facts and he will give up. This is known as challenging what you hear. Don't just believe it and sulk, challenge it with evidence.

Choice 3:

You can choose not to react. You can ignore the attacker which frustrates him. You already know what he said was not true so why should you care. Don't let what he says bother you. Just go on with your life. This way, you have chosen something helpful.

How to change depressing thoughts

Instead of saying "Today is such an awful day" try and say "What a wonderful day this is". This turns your negative thoughts into positive thoughts. This affects how you behave and feel. Instead of going back to bed and thinking more negative thoughts, you can pull the curtains whether snow is falling or not, whether it is gloomy or not, look through the window and expect the best.

Go and take a shower, dress up, take your breakfast and do constructive things such as going to work, doing household chores or going to college to further your career or helping others. This will make you feel better instead of staying in bed and feeling more depressed. It will in turn lead you to more positive thoughts that will make you feel better and better.

You need to be proactive and break the negative vicious cycle, either alone or with help from a therapist. Keep practicing. Once you master CBT you will influence how you feel and act on a daily basis.

Automatic thoughts

In this life we go through many events which our thoughts interpret or attach meaning to. The mind interprets what we see, hear, feel, smell and taste, differently. We taste a fruit and we can attach a meaning like sweet, sour, acidic or bitter to it. When we see the fruit, we associate it with the previous taste. This is the same with life's events. We give meaning to what happens according to our own interpretations.

We make judgments about all that is happening around us and label it like good or bad, easy or hard, safe or dangerous, pleasant or unpleasant and kind or mean. These judgments start during our childhood upbringing. There are kids who hate eating vegetables and they even fear the most harmless animals.

This goes on through life. We choose a subject in school and decide it is hard which in turn blocks our mind to other possibilities. We live with this mindset unless we decide to change. These meanings we attach to events or situations lead to our emotional feelings and physical sensations.

We feel happy or sad, relaxed or tired, hopeful or hopeless, happy or angry in addition to other inappropriate emotions such as fear, anxiety, depression, disappointment and frustration when applied in the wrong scenarios.

Belief systems

Different people give different meanings to the same events or situations.
This depends on their belief systems which are made up of:

- genes and personality traits
- childhood upbringing
- personal values
- culture
- past experiences
- religious beliefs
- no specific reasons

Many times we believe our thoughts without checking whether they are true or not. You may believe that someone at work hates you even though it may not be true.

You may believe that you cannot lose weight because you have tried several times before and failed. This is not true, but when you believe it, you stop trying to lose weight.

These thoughts are based on your past experiences and they keep repeating themselves until they set a persistent trend. These thoughts are not helpful.

Thinking habits that are not helpful

You need to identify thinking habits that are not helpful in order to get rid of them. You may be feeling sad over something that is not real. Maybe your friend passed you without saying "Hello". If you start thinking that she hates you, she does not care about you and she does not want to see you, then you are wrong.

Maybe she did not notice you. You may believe that you are overweight and you look unattractive. That is only in your mind. This may lead you to overeat and purge the food up or use laxatives. You may become so thin that everyone worries about you. These are unhelpful thoughts that could lead to depression.

Whatever it is that you are going through in life, challenge your thoughts and replace them with alternative thoughts that are helpful. Next time you see your friend; start a conversation by saying "Hi". Look at yourself in the mirror and self-talk to yourself how lovely you are.

Write affirmations that you will repeat over and over again every day regardless of what your problems you are having. You will lift up your spirits and your moods will change for the better. Remind yourself of your affirmations. Pin them on the wall in your office or bedroom and stick them on your fridge and believe in yourself.

Remember, no one will believe in you if you don't believe in yourself. No one will respect you if you don't respect yourself, and no one will love you if you don't love what you see in the mirror.

Alternative thoughts

You can change unhelpful thinking habits by being more realistic, more rational and looking at the problem from different perspectives.

Instead of thinking: she hates me

Think: she did not see me and that is why she passed by me without saying hello.

Instead of thinking: I cannot lose weight.

Think: I can lose weight if I keep trying.

Instead of thinking: I am a loser.

Think: I am good enough.

Replace unrealistic and unhelpful thoughts with realistic, balanced and rational thoughts that are positive. Balance your thoughts instead of being overly pessimistic or unreasonably optimistic.

Looking at something through different perspectives

You should look at the situation from many angles. Think about what a reasonable or rational person would do in similar situations. Be realistic and be rational as we shall see in Chapter 8.

6: How to Change Your Behavior

Behavioral therapy focuses on helping you understand how changing your behavior can lead to changes in your feelings. The goal of this behavioral therapy is to increase your engagement with other people so that you can be involved in positive and socially-reinforcing activities. Common behavioral techniques include:

- *Self-monitoring* - is the first stage of CBT treatment. You are asked to keep a diary or log of all your activities during the day. The therapist examines the list during your next session to see what you have been doing.

- *Scheduling of weekly activities* - you and your therapist will work together to schedule new activities for the following week.

- *Role playing* - helps you to develop new skills on social interactions based on what you anticipate.

- *Behavior modification* - to reinforce positive behavior, you receive a reward or you can reward yourself after engaging in positive behavior. Rewards will motivate you to change your behavior.

When you change what you do or your behavior, it affects how you think and how you feel.

There are many bad habits you can rectify with the help of CBT. Smoking, drugs, and alcohol may be destroying your life in many ways. It could lead to addictions, some types of cancer and self-harm.

You need stay determined when you set out to change your behavior because you will experience withdrawal symptoms that may discourage you. Tell your family and friends what you are doing so they can offer words of encouragement.

How to change your behavior

To change your behavior, you need to ask yourself several questions. Start by asking yourself:

- When I was faced with this same situation in the past how did I cope?
- What did I do and what did I not do?
- How did I go through that situation?
- What were my reactions?
- What were the consequences?
- How did my actions affect the way I felt?
- What could I have done differently?
- What would someone else have done differently in that same situation?

Think of someone you respect and ask yourself:

- If it was her, what could she have done or not done?
- What would have been the consequences?

You should also ask yourself:

- If I had paused or thought about it first, would I have done the same thing I did?
- How would have things turned out?

Think of the many options that you had and write them down and ask yourself:

- If I had tried these options, what difference would it have made?
- How would I have felt differently?
- How would I have thought differently?
- Would it have been more or less helpful?
- If I did things differently, what would have been the consequences?

Many times we are faced with situations that make us react without considering what the consequences of those actions would be. CBT helps us to think before we act. You need to practice several times, pausing for a moment and taking a deep breath before you act on a situation to help you see the whole thing clearly. Any time you are about to react, stop and take a deep breath. This will give you time to think about your actions and what consequences they may bring and how you can handle the situation differently to achieve better results. By taking a deep breath and pausing, you will have the option to consider which action you will take.

Consider all the options

Think about all the options available. How did you handle similar situations in the past? And how they turned out? How would other people in similar circumstances act? And then you take action. Make the right decisions and you will not regret it.

Look at all the options available and ask yourself:

- Is this the right choice?
- What will the consequence be?

Coping with mood disorders

Many times in your life you will be faced with a crisis. At such distressing times you may act involuntarily and regret it later. Try the following recommendations to cope with anxiety, depression and other conditions.

- Pause and take a breathe
- Relax
- Change your behavior by doing things differently from the way you normally do.

- Do other activities you enjoy that will divert your attention.
- Play calming music or your favorite music.
- Dance around.
- Do some exercises such as walking, swimming and jogging or go to the gym.
- Do things that are creative like painting, gardening or baking.
- Take your notebook and write down your feelings, thoughts, and anything that comes to your mind.
- Call a family member, friend or chat online.
- Visit a neighbor, family or a friend. They will be glad to see you and this will lift your moods and emotions.
- Reach out to others and help them.
- Have prayer or meditation.

Getting rid of addiction

You may have addictions that are hard to overcome

- Bulimia
- Alcohol and drug abuse
- Smoking

Alcohol abuse may affect your relationships, your quality of life and loss of control. It can lead to health problems such as alcohol poisoning, cirrhosis of the liver, and loss of close relationships. It can also lead to destructive behaviors such as drinking and driving, violence and self-harm. Long-term alcohol abuse may lead to heart disease, stroke, liver cancer and bowel cancer. On top of these, you may lose personal property like wallets, mobile phones, keys and other property. Alcohol abuse has been a contributory factor to domestic violence, divorce, unemployment, anxiety, stress and depression.

You can change this behavior by making the right choices.

7: Overcoming Mood Disorders and Addictions

The first step in overcoming mood disorders, addictions, or any other psychological problems is to know more about it. You should know how and why it is affecting your life. By doing this, you pave the way to recovery and find solutions and solve the problems either on your own or with help. You may find that having a better understanding of what you are going through is a leap towards recovery.

Relaxation strategies

When you are going through stressful situations your muscles tense up, you get chest pains and you breathe with difficulty. You may feel dizzy and experience extreme fatigue. You need to learn how to relax your whole body by doing deep breathing and calm breathing exercises. These exercises are a helpful part of cognitive behavioral therapy.

You need to practice the following relaxation techniques:

- deep breathing exercises involves inhaling deeply, holding the breathe and exhaling

- calm breathing means breathing in and breathing out slowly
- progressive muscle relaxation means tensing any group of muscles and relaxing them
- other relaxation methods include prayer and meditation

How to overcome anxiety disorders

CBT is a useful treatment for anxiety disorders. Patients who experience persistent panic attacks are encouraged to test out their beliefs that may be causing such attacks. These may include specific fears related to bodily sensations and developing more realistic responses to these experiences. This is beneficial in decreasing both the frequency and intensity of panic attacks. Patients who experience obsessions, compulsions, and fear are guided to expose themselves in a safe and controlled therapeutic environment.

The same is true for people with phobias, including phobias of animals or phobias of evaluation by others (termed as social anxiety disorder). Those patients who are receiving treatment are exposed to what they fear most gradually. The beliefs that have served to maintain those fears are targeted for modification. CBT is often referred to as a first line treatment for many long-term conditions that require specialized treatment.

How to overcome depression

If you have depression you may look out through the window and say "This is such an awful day." This is unlike someone else who says "What a wonderful day this is." If you think the day is awful, it will most likely be that way. This is because instead of taking a shower, eating breakfast and getting ready for the day, you may decide to stay in bed a little longer which makes you feel even more depressed. When you maintain the same thoughts, feelings and actions, you continue to stay depressed. CBT helps you to break that vicious cycle from negative thoughts to positive ones.

CBT breaks down the vicious cycle into different parts. This way, you are able to deal with each part and change it on your own. You can find ways to tackle your problems with or without the help of a trained therapist.

It is true that you cannot change some situations but you can change the way you feel about them. The therapist will help you tackle your problems by changing your negative thoughts to improve the way you feel. With time, you are able to achieve this on your own without the help of a therapist.

What is exposure therapy?

Exposure therapy is a type of CBT used for people who have phobia, panic attacks and obsessive compulsive behavior. These people may not get all the help they need from talking treatment. They may talk about it, but they are made to face their fears by being in a controlled therapeutic environment to help them cope.

How to overcome panic attacks

Panic attacks can overwhelm you with anxiety and fear. Patients who experience persistent panic attacks are encouraged to see a therapist. Beliefs surrounding their fears (of contamination, illness, inflicting harm, etc.) are identified and changed to decrease the anxiety connected with such fears.

In exposure therapy, you first start with situations that cause your anxiety. Your therapist will ask you which anxieties you can tolerate. You are encouraged to stay in that situation for about 1-2 hours or until the anxiety starts to decrease significantly.

When you are exposed to something that you fear for a prolonged time, you start getting used to it. After the first session, your therapist will encourage you to repeat the exposure exercise about 3 times a day. At first, you may feel the same as before, but after being exposed a few times, you will realize your anxiety and fear is really not much at all. You should move from one situation to another until you have conquered all your anxieties and fears.

How to Overcome Phobia

What are you anxious about? Is it spiders, heights or water? You may have been born with these fears or you may have developed them through your bad experiences. To untangle these phobias or obsessive compulsive disorders (OCD) you need to be taken through these situations in a methodical and structured way. This is what exposure therapy is about.

Take for example phobia of water. Because you had an unpleasant experience with water, you avoid swimming at all costs. For whatever reason you always believe whenever you are near water, you will surely drown. Your therapist exposes you to water while at the same time modifies the beliefs that have maintains such fears.

How to overcome addictions:

Substance addictions

When people have addictions, it means they have a strong needs and desires for which they cannot control. Addictions include those related to foods, alcohol and drugs. They take substances to be the most important thing in their life not realizing that it can affect not only their lives but others also.

Drinking alcohol, smoking, taking substances and gambling can lead to long-term problems.
CBT has been found to be helpful in treating various forms of addictions and breaking these unhealthy habits. Talking therapy like cognitive behavioral therapy and at times medications are recommended to treat addictions.

Bulimia nervosa

Bulimia nervosa is an eating disorder that makes people eat and then purge up the food. This condition may be caused by low self-esteem and depression, among other causes. CBT is effective in treating bulimia nervosa and you can apply it either on your own or by asking a family member or a friend to work with you.

8: Changing Your Perspective

Many thoughts that come across our minds are based on opinions instead of facts. There is a story about an elephant. Five blind people were sent to observe an elephant. One person touched the ears and reported back and said that, the elephant was like a fan. Another one touched the legs and reported that it was like a building pole. The third one touched the side of the elephant and concluded that it was like a wall. The other one touched the trunk and said that it was like a snake while the fifth one touched the tusk and reported that it was hard and firm. You can see how people differ about the same thing.

Looking at different perspectives

There are many different perspectives to one thing. That is why in a court of justice, the judge or jury calls many witnesses, lawyers/advocates and prosecutors to give evidence. Each one of them gives evidence based on what they saw, heard and felt about the event or situation.

We may look at something and make our own judgments about it without looking from different perspectives. At first it may seem one way, but if we take time to explore other possibilities we may end up with different facts and opinions about the whole thing.

We attach different meanings to situations, events, interactions, conversations and all that is happening to us, around us, to others and to the world. Instead of seeing things the way they are, we make our own interpretations about them.

You need to be realistic about what you are going through? Do you need to drink alcohol? Do you have to smoke? Why are you overeating? What purpose will it serve? How will this affect you? What are the consequences?

You should be rational and ask yourself what would someone else (you respect) do if faced with the same situation?

Learn to view things differently

You should view things at wider perspectives, what is known as "seeing the bigger picture." Stand back and see the "bigger picture." You may be entangled in negative emotions which make you irrational.

Try to balance your moods with your rational thoughts. Apply your reasonable mind (based on facts) to what you are going through. This way you will be able to respond to what is going on in the most helpful and effective way.

Someone might attack you with words. What will you do? The first reaction is to do the same to him. But does it help? We say that two wrongs don't make a right. In fact, you feel your moods overwhelm you by doing the wrong thing.

Swallow your pride and think about it first. You may feel like you are choking with anger but doing the right thing will ultimately lift your spirits. You will feel happier for making the right decision.

We all have different belief systems and how you might see a situation may be different from the way I see it. Think about how other people might see the situation differently. Since you may be overwhelmed by emotions, it is good for you to consider other people's perspectives (those who are not affected by these emotions).

Things to consider

Ask yourself:

- Am I dealing with facts or opinions?
- How am I reacting to this situation?
- How am I interpreting the situation? What meaning am I giving it?
- How can I look at it differently?
- How would others who are not emotionally affected see it? What meaning would they give? How would they react?
- What is the best thing to do?
- Are the thoughts I have helpful or unhelpful?

- What is the bigger picture?
- What is the best way of looking at it?
- If I was an outside, how would I look at it?

When you look at the situation in another perspective your moods will improve and this will lead to more healthy behavior. Your interactions and relationships will improve. Your self-esteem will improve and you will be more confident and see things in a realistic way.

You will look at people and situations differently. You will be able to communicate more effectively and treat others with empathy. You will feel better about yourself and be happier.

The best thing about CBT is you can adjust your mind and your behavior so that your moods and emotions can change for the better. To influence the way we react, we need to change our minds to positive, rational and realistic thoughts.

Considering Facts vs. Opinions

Many times opinions are mistaken for facts leading people to make the wrong choices. A fact is based on evidence. It is the truth and nothing can change that. No one can dispute a fact because it is based on rational thoughts. We all have our own opinions about ourselves, about others, about situations and the world at large.

Opinions are based on personal views and our belief systems. These can vary depending on the individual's upbringing, family values, and level of education, knowledge, past experiences, religious beliefs, culture, personality traits, and personal values. They also depend on current circumstances because you may have different opinions about the same thing at different times.

For example, you may change your opinions as you grow older. Opinions vary from one person to another and each person is entitled to his or her opinion. When we are stressed, distressed or frightened we have irrational thoughts that are not true. Stress makes us more irrational because we act on emotions and opinions we have. Two people can be faced with the same situation and end up with different opinions about the whole thing.

These opinions fuel emotions and emotions reinforce opinions. That is why it is important to ask ourselves "is this a fact or an opinion?", when we are faced with mood disorders or addictions.

Take for example obsessive compulsive behavior. This is a combination of obsessive thinking and compulsive behavior. You may have overwhelming thoughts that you might be attacked which makes you more alert. You start looking around expecting to be attacked. This is followed by compulsive behavior such as walking faster, having palpitations, fiddling with your bag, shopping in places you believe are more secure and avoiding contacts with people.

You should stop and ask yourself whether you are dealing with facts or opinions.

- Are these thoughts facts or opinions?
- What is the truth?
- Why do you think you might be attacked?
- What do you know?

Deal with these thoughts and if there is nothing factual, dismiss them. Do not allow your opinions to strengthen your emotions and do not allow your emotions to intensify your opinions because it could lead to long-term problems. Don't allow opinions to distress you.

On the other hand, if you are basing your thoughts on facts, then you need to make the right choices. Take the best action possible. Make wise decisions about what you will do.

9: Adopting Lifestyle Changes to prevent a relapse

You have worked so hard on your mood disorders and addictions and still find yourself relapsing. CBT is like any other skill that needs to be managed. Practice your skills on a daily basis. Make it a good habit to keep doing what is helpful and avoid what is not. Sometimes you may slip back into your old habits but you should not beat yourself up if you are determined to overcome your problems.

The worst thing you can do is give up because you will lose all the improvements that you have made. When you learn new strategies of overcoming your problems, you should not allow yourself to fall into a relapse. Of course, you may have a lapse at one time or another which is normal but a relapse should be avoided by all means.

Difference between a lapse and a relapse

A lapse is a short-term return to those old habits. This is normal. A relapse is completely returning to your old ways of addictions, thinking and behaving in unhelpful ways and feeling the same as you felt before you learned the new CBT strategies. While it is quite normal for patients to experience lapses now and then, relapse should be avoided.

How to prevent lapses and relapses

Practice

Practice your CBT skills daily and keep practicing. Keep a log of your activities and achievements for self-monitoring.

Write down your course of action

Write a list of what you will do every day or every week and stick to it. This way, you will prevent a relapse because now you know what you are supposed to do. Practice regularly and you will find it easier to handle any situations that arise.

Be aware of what might cause a lapse or relapse

Try to find out when you are likely to have a lapse or relapse. These are times when you are very vulnerable. Be proactive and act before it happens. Take measures that will help you stay on course of what you are doing and you will be less likely to have a lapse or relapse.

Become focused and promise yourself that you will soldier on whatever challenges that come ahead of you. Without determination you will fall back so become determined and stay focused. Set goals that you want to achieve and break them into smaller goals that are achievable.

Notice the warning signs

Make a list of the warning signs and avoid them. If you start having negative thoughts or start arguing with people, then you know you have become anxious. These are red flags that need to be corrected immediately! List down the warning signs and when you notice you have them, practice CBT skills such as calm breathing or deep breathing exercises or challenge your negative thoughts and replace them with helpful ones. You can also prevent further future lapses by being more alert and handling new challenges as they arise. Always remember that you are the one in control.

Take control

Keep working, don't stop. If you do, new challenges will take over. Try to figure out what happened and take control of the situation that led you fall back to old habits. Always have a plan of how you will cope with the difficult situations that present themselves in the future. Have a Plan A and Plan B in place so that if one does not work you can adopt the other one. Do not blame yourself so much because lapses are normal and you can learn a lot from them.

Lifestyle changes

Make other lifestyle changes that will help you in your journey towards full recovery.

- Eat healthy – you should eat a healthy diet that is comprised of fresh fruits and vegetables, whole grains, healthy fats, natural sweeteners (if you like sugar) and healthy juices, smoothies and salads. Avoid foods like refined sugar, saturated fats, trans-fats and processed foods loaded with refined sugar, additives, colorings and preservatives.

- Exercise regularly – walking, jogging, running, swimming, hiking and aerobic exercises are all good for you.

- Relax and sleep – have a good night's sleep and learn to relax.

- Drink plenty of pure drinking water.

We all want to live happily and this is possible when you practice the principles recommended in this book. Mood disorders and addictions affect our joy and the joy of those around us. You now know that whatever the problem may be, you can change it and encourage others to do the same.

This way, your joy will reflect on them and their joy will reflect back to you. There is nothing that you cannot change, whether they are your thoughts, feelings or behaviors because they are linked to each other.

Don't sit back; take steps that will make you a better person and you will be glad that you took that bold step.

Conclusion

Changing thoughts and behavior, as stated in this book, is a helpful way to alleviate mood disorders and addictions. If you can apply the principles recommended in this book and eat healthy foods and exercise the CBT skills regularly, you will overcome the challenges that prevent you from enjoying your life and having a meaningful life.

"Cognitive Behavioral Therapy: *For All Mood Disorders and Addictions*" is a must-read book for anyone who has mood disorders and addictions. Research studies have proved that. CBT is effective in the treatment of mental illnesses and many other conditions. In fact, CBT has been found to be more effective than medications in some instances.

www.ingramcontent.com/pod-product-compliance
Lightning Source LLC
Chambersburg PA
CBHW070817290526
45795CB00002B/743